'A Decapitated Coffee, Please'
and other great malapropisms

'A Decapitated Coffee, Please'

and other great malapropisms

Des MacHale

MERCIER PRESS

Mercier Press
Douglas Village, Cork
www.mercierpress.ie

Trade enquiries to Columba Mercier Distribution,
55a Spruce Avenue, Stillorgan Industrial Park, Blackrock,
Dublin

Illustrations by Joe Gervin
1 85635 492 X

10 9 8 7 6 5 4 3 2 1

the arts
council
schomhairle
ealaíon

Mercier Press receives financial assistance from
the Arts Council/An Chomhairle Ealaíon

Printed in Ireland by ColourBooks

Introduction

You have no idea how excited I was to discover, while searching through my ancestral files, the papers of my great-great-grand-aunt, Mrs Vagina Malaprop. She was so famous that she appeared in a play called *The Rivals*, written by Richard Bramley Sheridan (1751–1816) in 1775. The family name appears to be derived from the French *mal à propos*, meaning an inappropriate remark or 'ill to the purpose'.

My ancestor's name has now become an established part of the English language and she is as anonymous as the hoover, Kleenex and coke. In plain language, a malapropism is the replacing of one word by another of like sound or form but radically different meaning, which often conjures up a totally different image from the one intended. The best malapropisms are those where the new unintended meaning is often a more appropriate description of the situation. For example, Mrs Malaprop might state that her moth-eaten old fur coat was bought at a 'jungle sale'. In general, the listener is aware of the malapropism but the speaker is not. They are an excellent illustration of Edgar Allan Poe's dictum – a little learning is a dangerous thing.

Malapropisms occur most often with longer technical words derived from the Latin or Greek and are more common since the decline of the study of the classical languages in school. They are rife in medicine, science, literature and foreign languages and in fact in any technical area where the layman or laywoman blunders in.

5

Why do so many people find malapropisms so funny? One reason may be that they make us feel very superior – after all, we would never make the silly verbal mistakes poor old Mrs Malaprop makes – or would we?

Secondly, they illustrate the extraordinary richness of the language, revealing hidden connections between words and concepts, just as dreams do – just imagine Mrs Malaprop wearing her Freudian slip.

Thirdly, the vast majority of them are authentic, much too good to have been manufactured, and reality has the uncanny knack of being a lot funnier than anything fiction can contrive.

Finally, the malapropism is a first cousin of the Irish Bull, the blunder, the blooper, the boner, the howler, the slip of the tongue, where many a true word is spoken in jest.

This book contains over seven hundred malapropisms – the biggest collection that has ever been assembled. They have all come from the mouth of Mrs Malaprop and her many descendants and in her honour I have chosen to report them all in her words. But keep your ears open and you will hear many more of them, because a descendant of Mrs Malaprop is living near you.

Des MacHale
Cork, 2006

I took a first-aid course and because I like to try out my skills on real patients, I got a part-time job with our local ambulance service. One night we were called out in an emergency to an old man who had just been involved in a fire, but unfortunately, before the ambulance arrived, the old man died. What a pity we didn't arrive in time or I could have resuffocated and survived him.

My doctor has just gone on holiday and left a locust to take over his practice.

I just love the smell of freshly baked bread. As I always say, too many cooks make an ill wind.

I remember very well my first helicopter flight. I was delighted to be back on terracotta again.

I don't really believe in the claims of alternative medicine. I'm a confirmed septic in such matters.

I've been reading a very interesting book about General Rommel who commanded Hitler's Pansy Division in North Africa.

I'm sorry my father wasn't a surgeon because when I went to the hospital I would have been given the RIP treatment.

I am not divorced but I am enstrangled from my husband.

I have a big blank wall at the side of my house and I'm thinking of having a Muriel painted on it to brighten it up.

My doctor once refused to treat me because I didn't have enough money to pay him. What about the hypocritical oath he swore when he qualified?

I've been reading a terrific book about a Soviet agent who defecated to the west.

Who was that famous man who was prime minister of India?
Bandit Nehru wasn't it?

My little daughter has just gone off to boarding school for the first time so I've put her entrails on all her underwear.

My telephone bill is at least twice as much as it should be. I've a good mind to write to the omnibusman.

I'm not superstitious but I like to read my horrorscope in the newspaper every day.

My father was a wonderful musician. He played the baboon in a sympathy orchestra.

Between you and me, I've never really like my surname Malaprop. I'm thinking of having it changed by Interpol.

I remember once when I went on holiday and got the fright of my life in the Sea Shells. I was swimming in the sea when a big octobus came out of the water and wrapped his testicles around me.

My son sent me a lovely bottle of Bowjelly for Christmas so I sent him a little note saying 'I am internally grapeful for the whine'.

My cat has just died so I had better bury it before vigour mortis sets in.

My husband can do virtually anything around the house. He a Jekyll of all trades.

I'll never forget the time I was a patient in a public ward in a hospital and the woman in the bed next to me had an apologetic fit.

My favourite international politician was Yasser Marrowfat, who did so much for the peas process.

MY RELIGIOUS BELIEFS

Jesus was betrayed by Judas the carrycot.

Jesus was condemned by a bunch of spiders.

And the angel said 'Take the child and flea into Egypt'.

The pope lives in a vacuum.

The Holy Ghost, the parakeet, descended on the apostles.

Jesus cured the ten leprechauns.

Moses went up Mount Cyanide and came down with ten tabloids of stone.

And Jesus said 'Blessed are the cheesemakers'.

At the last supper, the apostles drank so much they were filled with the holy spirit.

Jesus had a lady friend called Mary Mandolin.

When I pray I always say, 'Blessed art thou a monk's women'.

And the angel said to Mary, 'Hail, highly flavoured one'.

The bible tells us not to lay up trousers on earth.

The Wise Men brought gifts of gold, Frankenstein and myrrh.

My favourite animal in religion is the prairie tortoise – Mindful of our Saviour's bidding and of the prairie tortoise.

Mary was exposed to a man named Joseph.

Judas Asparagus was one of the twelve apostles.

Salami demanded the head of John the Blacklist.

Jews worship in a cinemagogue.

The pope is inflammable.

In Greek Orthodox churches they burn insects.

The principal religion of Iran is Muslin.

The Children of Israel spent forty years wandering through the dessert.

Joseph had a goat of many colours.

Jacob, the son of Isaac, stole his brother's birthmark.

Solomon had five hundred wives and seven hundred cucumbers.

When Catholics die they are purified in purgatives.

God spoke to Moses from a burning bus.

Salome danced naked in front of Harrods.

Pontius Pilot captained the flight into Egypt.

This is how the burial service goes – In the name of the Father and of the Son and into the hole he goes.

The first book in the bible is the Book of Guinnesses.

Round John virgin, mother and child.

Angels lie prostate before the Lord.

The child Jesus was persecuted by King Horrid.

It is not awful to marry your brother's wife.

Deliver us from e-mail and men.

Protestants do not like the smell of incest in Catholic churches.

John the Baptist was beheaded with the axe of the apostles.

The smell from the drains was driving me crazy so I sent for the sanity inspector.

I'm afraid I'm spending a lot of time in the bathroom at the moment. I have an attack of dire rear.

My husband, who is a drummer, went on strike recently and the entire band came out in symphony.

There was a night watchman keeping guard over the roadworks outside my house one night. It was very frosty but I wasn't worried about him because he kept himself warm with a burning brassiere.

My neighbour has just bought an expensive new car. It even has a Catholic converter.

My son has just got a job with a top firm. He's a big clog in their machine.

I just love the TV series Big Bother.

My favourite explorer of all time is Mark O'Polo who travelled to the orient and brought the mint back to Europe.

I just love the way that the people of India dress – those lovely coloured turbines on their heads.

My son and his girlfriend have just set out on a continental touring holiday on one of those tantrum bicycles.

I have given up arguing with my husband. He is totally imprevious to logic.

My nephew is planning a military career. He intends to join the Gherkins in India.

I believe that violence just begets violence and the whole thing becomes a viscous circle.

I once attended a play were the costumes and makeup were very realistic. Two actors were dressed in the garbage of monk and they even went so far as to cut real tonsils on their head.

I was very worried when I was told that my husband the musician had a tuba on his brain but thank heavens it turned out to be non-militant.

I was staying in a convent in San Francisco when an earthquake hit. I woke up to find beside me a yawning abbess.

My uncle has just returned from the African jungle, full of the most wonderful antidotes supplied by the natives.

I would love to fly from London to Edinburgh on the new shuffle service.

I once had to reprimand my little boy for removing a buggy from his nose with his finger.

Once, when I was in court, the judge asked who was making the allegations and I told him that I was the alligator.

Whenever I buy a furniture flatpack I never begin to assemble it until I have read the destructions thoroughly.

I am very proud of my son's recent government job. He has just been appointed an inspector in the Departure from Education.

My daughter has been attending a cookery course in a famous French school of cousin. She gravitated top of her class and was awarded the condom blue.

My father used to collect stamps but he gave it up when he remembered the old proverb 'Philately will get you nowhere'.

I'm not going to go to any more political meetings. Last time I attended one, soufflés broke out in the crowd.

Last summer my husband and I stayed in a big city hotel. What impressed me most was the revolting door at the front.

I've been helping my daughter furnish her new house. I bought her a pelvis on which to hang her curtains.

From an early age my son wanted a career in law enforcement, so he became a defective in the police farce.

For the cold winter ahead I intend to infest in some terminal underwear.

My son has just given his girlfriend a well-deserved maternity ring.

I know I'm inclined to gossip a bit but that is no reason for my neighbours to stop speaking to me. In fact a few of them have ostrichised me.

I've very afraid of being attacked by a stranger some dark night so I'm taking a course in the marital arts.

I don't like the way my little granddaughter speaks so I'm paying for her to have a course of electrocution lessons.

I'd love to take a keep-fit course because I fancy myself in one of those leopard outfits.

I don't really like going upstairs in big department stores because I'm afraid of travelling on the alligators.

I prefer to do my Christmas shopping in November because then I don't have to mangle with the terrible crowds.

At one stage my musician husband used to play the hobo in an orchestra.

I'm afraid my husband will run off with another woman. I don't want to be involved in an infernal triangle.

I do not approve of unmarried couples corabbiting together.

The first time I saw a nudist I was quite shocked. There he was standing starch naked on the beach.

My Theatrical Career

In 1775 the famous playright Mr Richard Bramley Sheridan wrote a wonderful play called The Rivals *and wrote a part especially for me. Here are some of the lines I had but I'm afraid some of them suffer from being out of contact:*

But the point we would request of you is that you will promise to forget this fellow, to illiterate him, I say, quite from your memory.

Now don't attempt to extirpate yourself from the matter; you know I have proof of it.

Nay, nay, Sir Anthony, you are an absolute misanthropy.

Fie, fie, Sir Anthony, you surely speak laconically.

Well, at any rate I shall be glad to get her from my intuition.

But mind, Lucy, if ever you betray what you are encrusted with (unless it be other people's secrets to me) you forfeit my malevolence for ever.

But from the ingenuity of your appearance, I am convinced you deserve the character here given of you.

He is the very pineapple of politeness.

But, behold, this very day I have interceded another letter from the fellow.

Then he's so well bred, so full of alacrity and adulation.

Well, Sir Anthony, since you desire it, we will not anticipate the past.

That gentleman can tell you – 'twas he enveloped the affair to me.

You have no more feeling than one of the Derbyshire petrifactions.

Why, fly with the utmost felicity.

Nay, no delusions to the past.

Oh, he will dissolve my mystery.

I am as headstrong as an allegory on the banks of the Nile.

In my English class in school, I learned about the bowels, which are a, e, i, o and u.

In prostitution it is not the call girls who are at fault but the pimples who take all of their money.

I'm not going to the Middle East. I might get bitten by a mad dog and go down with rabbis.

I have written a serious novel but I do not expect to have it published in my lifetime. However, there is a good chance that it may appear posthumorously.

I don't get on very well with my next-door neighbour. I don't like her and she doesn't like me, so the feeling is entirely neutral.

My daughter got married recently though not in a church. It was one of those off-licence places.

We should all be kind to illiterate children – after all it's not their fault their parents weren't married.

The police picked up my son once on suspicion of burglary but he had a cast iron ali baba that he was somewhere else at the time.

I went out to dinner recently and the first item on the menu was the dreaded cutlet.

I don't take risks for other people. I'm not putting my head in a moose for anybody.

I think most university students are crazy – non campus mentis.

My sister never married. She remained a sphincter all her life.

I just love chicken, turkey and other foul dinners.

I once saw a very disturbing war film in which a Japanese soldier committed Mata Hari.

I went to the doctor and he injected me with an epidemic needle.

I went to the supermarket and bought a cartoon of orange juice.

Our local store went on strike and it was closed for altercations.

Ancient Greek poets were inspired by the tragic mouse.

I'm hoping to go to Africa for my annual vaccination.

I have great sympathy for people in jail. If one escaped, I'd give him refuse in my house.

My father wanted to join a circus but his parents forbade it. All his life he had a chimp on his shoulder because of that.

I have a great admiration for stormtroopers who break down doors, rush into buildings and release ostriches.

I find I can no longer read the face of my old watch so I have decided to buy one of those new genital watches.

The apple I bought recently had a dirty great magnet at the core.

I have an abbess on my gums which makes eating nearly impossible.

Between you and me I like the odd little drink so I'm glad I didn't live in America during proposition.

One of the best boxing matches I ever saw was Cassius Clay vice versa Sonny Liston.

The first and second things I want in life are security and fame respectably.

My mother-in-law is seriously ill. She collapsed and is still in a comma.

I was given a present of a lovely new pen for my birthday, so now I can write in hysterics.

I have been called the matron saint of all verbal blunderers.

I was taking part in a quiz and the first question I was asked was: 'What did Socrates die of?'
I promptly replied 'An overdose of wedlock'.

I lost my first job as a secretary because of bad punctuation. This was very unfair as I was always at work every morning at nine o' clock on the dot.

My next-door neighbour goes in and out to the city to work every day. He's a computer.

I believe in capital punishment for children in schools as long as it's not too severe.

I went for a walk in the countryside one summer's evening and was nearly eaten alive by midgets. I wish I had brought some insect propellant with me.

My daughter is getting married next week so she is busily preparing her torso.

If animals ever attack us we should fight back with gorilla warfare.

I've been reading a very sad book about the Russian Revolution. The Bolsheviks murdered the Czar and all the little Sardines.

Here is a good household tip – if your bread is stale you can toast it under the gorilla.

I just love that Latin proverb – *De mortuis nihil nisi bonum* – In dead people you'll find nothing but bones.

When invaders came, ancient tribes used to light a deacon on top of a hill to warn others.

The customs man accused me of having pornography in my luggage. I told him not to be ridiculous – I haven't even got a pornograph to play it on.

SCIENCE

Radio was invented by Macaroni.

A thermometer is measured in centipede.

A force twelve torpedo is very destructive.

The amoeba is a one-celled orgasm.

Atoms join together to form monocles.

A triangle with an angle bigger than 90^0 is called obscene.

Each drop of water contains millions of Germans.

The longest side of a right-angled triangle is called a hippopotamus.

Lemons commit mass suicide by jumping over cliffs.

Juniper is the largest of the planets.

A Mammon is a type of elephant found in the bible.

A Stradivarius was a type of ancient dinosaur.

A centimetre is an insect with a hundred legs.

Hard water is well-frozen ice.

Einstein's Law of Relatives can be summed up in the simple equation $E = H_2O$.

180^0 is the boiling point of a triangle.

Pythagoras was the first man to breed a hypotenuse in captivity.

Hot water is H_2O and cold water is CO_2.

Menstruation is the art of measurement.

Pasteur discovered the Milky Way.

Radium was discovered by Madman Curry.

Irrelevant is an animal that lives in Africa.

The first Nobell Prize was won by the man who invented the silent alarm clock.

I'm not very good at mathematics – I've never even mastered the dismal system.

The earth makes a complete resolution every twenty-four hours.

The volt is called after Voltaire who first invented electricity.

I was so surprised you could have knocked me down with a fender.

I don't like to eat food with too many conservatives in it.

I just love those television clerics who tell jokes – Knickerless Parsons.

To kill flies nothing is more efficient than an old-fashioned swastika.

I love those old-fashioned novels where the hero wears a molecule in his eye.

I have just bought a pair of those wonderful waterproof knickers they use in the continent.

If you want to stay slim, chew each piece of food thirty-two times – masturbate, masturbate, masturbate!

When a man with evil designs on me tried to seduce me, I reclined to do so.

A good public speaker should always breathe with his diagram.

My little daughter has just failed her third spelling test in a row. I'm afraid she may be anorexic.

My mother has lost her memory completely. She's suffering from Tunisia.

I believe in marriage. Men and women have always had a very strong infinity for each other.

I like to follow the Stock Exchange. I read the Davy Jones Index every day.

My new car has some wonderful features. It's a hunch-back.

I was on television recently and had a fine old time in the hostility room.

If I want to find something I just look up the ibex at the back of the book.

When I was little I used to play with my doll and imagine I was a Red Indian lady. I was the squawk and my doll was the squawker or the caboose.

I love to pick damsels fresh from the trees.

One of my favourite composers is Mows Art and I admire him particularly because he was an infant podgy.

I am an animal lover. I do not believe that wild beasts should be confined in theological gardens.

I went on a tour of a medieval church recently. I was very impressed by the flying buttocks in the design.

Low air fares are a blessing in the sky.

If someone makes veiled suggestions about me I always ask them what they are incinerating.

I have just bought a new dog. He's a cocky spaniel.

One of my greatest pleasures in life is to have a giraffe of wine with a good meal.

At my father's funeral, the coffin was carried by six polar bears.

The first time I met my husband he invited me upstairs to see his itchings.

I'd love to own a Siamese cat but I could never afford to feed the two of them.

I'm very upset that my daughter has become a streetwalking protestant.

I think the law is too laxative on criminals.

I would like to become an American citizen but because I wasn't born there they would have to neutralise me first.

I do a bit of sailing on the river and I always keep a boat tied up at the dwarf.

I married young in the first fine careless rupture of love.

MY FAVOURITE SONGS AND MUSIC

Feed the Worms (Bob Gelding)

The Ants are my Friends (Rob Dillon)

Deck the Halls with Buddy Holly

I've Thrown a Custard on her Face

The Marriage of Fig Roll (Mow's Art)

Massinet's Medications

We Can Sing Full Though We Be

The Daring Young Man on the Flying Trapezium

Ruby Tanyard

O God Dour Help in Ages Past

Raindrops Keep Falling on my Bed

Stars and Strikes Forever

I'm a Dreamer, Montreal

Sam and Janet Evening

Wendy Red Red Robin Comes Bob Bob Bobbin' Along

Your Walrus Hurt the One You Love

Just a Pong at Toilet

Gladly the Cross-Eyed Bear

While Shepherds Washed their Socks by Night

I Left My Heart with Some Franciscans

Handel's Larger

Haydn's Cremation

Verdi's Rectum

Piddler on the Roof

Wagner's Ride of the Vultures

Puccini's Madam Buttermilk

The Maypole Leaf Forever

All Teachers Great and Small

Beethoven's Erotica Symphony

Rogers and Hammersmith's The Hounds of Munich

South Specific

Elgar's Enema Variations

Carry Me Back to Old Virginity

The King and Di

The Song is Ended but the Malady Lingers On

Verdi's Hyena

Andrew Lloyd Weber's Ryvita

Jesus Wants Me for a Sardine

Debussy's La Mal de Mer

The Dream of Geronimo

Rumpelstiltskin's Symphony

Tarzan Stripes Forever

Tchaikovsky's Pathetic Symphony

The Star-Spangled Banana

Hairy with the Light Brown Jeans

Rock Manninoff

Can't Get Loose to Using You

Hark the Harold Angles Sing

The Slurry with the Fridge on Top

The Blue Daniel Waltz

A weigh in a manger, no crib for a bed,
The little lord Jesus lay down his wee Ted.

The feast of All Hollows

Silent Night, Deadly Night

Bidet's Carmen

Big Horse I Love You

Hook and Eye Forget You

The London Derriere

Young girls should not always be blamed for se-ducing married men. I always say it takes two to tangle.

There are a lot of things I could say about a lot of people but I don't care to cast nasturtiums.

If ever I have a valuable document I always make a thermostat copy of it in case I lose it.

I may not be very good at grandma but at least I can puncture a sentence.

My grandfather was a solicitor and as a little girl I often visited his office. I can still smell the dusty lodgers he kept on a shelf in his office.

The train on which I was travelling recently was delayed when somebody pulled the excommunication cord.

One of my sons is training to be a doctor. Eventually, he hopes to become a sturgeon.

The traffic congestion near my house is unbelievable. I wish the council would build a dual cabbageway.

The wheels have just fallen off the base of my couch. It is very inconvenient pushing a castrated couch around.

I've just bought a new house. It's got a nine hundred and ninety-nine year leash.

At the end of the Second World War we had a VD party in our street.

I've just had a new kitchen installed in my house. It's even got a spit level grill.

A friend of mine will trace your family history for a very reasonable fee. He's a top-class gynaecologist.

I was in a rush the other morning and forgot to take my antideclamatory pills.

I just love the great outdoors especially using a camping stove run on profane gas.

The man in the shoe shop refused to refund my money because my shoes turned out to be too tight. I was very angry with him – as they say, 'Hell hath no fury like a woman's corns'.

Multiple births run in my family – my aunt had three culprits and my cousins had quadrupeds.

Alcohol was discovered by men living in the stoned age.

The income tax people insist that I owe them a huge amount of money but I think they owe me money. Both of us refuse to budget.

If my husband doesn't stop doing abdominal things to me in front of my friends, I swear I'll leave him.

A few years ago I was nearly drowned at the seaside. Fortunately, a lifeguard rescued me and gave me artificial insemination.

I'd love to go on a shooting holiday in Scotland. Maybe I could bag a few peasants.

I much prefer my old gramophone and my old 78 records. I don't like those new compost discs at all.

I find it very convenient to buy eggs in a cartoon.

I'm planning to take up art classes so I have bought myself a weasel.

My mother-in-law never seems to look a day older. She seems to have discovered the secret of eternal euthanasia.

The lawn of my Spanish house has Esperanto grass.

A certain actor I know claims to be a sexagenarian. At his age, I think that's disgusting.

I don't approve of universities where young men and women are forced to matriculate together.

When I visited the zoo recently, my favourite animals were the turquoises moving slowly in their cage.

My daughter has just given birth to a baby. To mark this suspicious event I'm going to present her with a silver tanker.

I've just been reading a book about the Kennedy assignation. I believe the fatal shot was fired by Lee Harvey Oswald from a Dallas Book Suppository.

I always hope for the best – I'm an eternal octopus.

I don't want my cat to have any more kittens so I'm having it sprayed.

I don't know what to do. I'm in a complete quarry.

You probably won't believe this, but I sometimes find it difficult to extinguish between different words.

I'm thinking of paying a visit to the chiropractor because I have a bazooka on my foot.

I can write with both left and right hands. I'm completely amphibious.

I'm very upset because a new blot of flats is being built just opposite my house.

One of the houses in my street is imputed to be haunted by a ghost. I think it should be taken out and exercised.

Politically, I'm a socialite. I believe that everyone should have a higher per capital income. When I see the rich getting away with paying no taxes, I think that is absolutely tantamount.

I'm often in trouble. I'm always jumping from the pancake into the frying pan.

I've just bought an expensive new pet – it's a filigree hamster.

Very overweight people should ipso fatso be refused medical treatment.

On my holiday in Scotland I bought a lovely new coat of haggis tweed.

My Medical Knowledge

The circulatory system contains the veins, the archeries and the caterpillars.

Consternation is when you haven't been to the toilet for a week.

Bodies are sent to a mortuary to be mortgaged.

Some doctors are eye and rear specialists.

If you can't eat in hospital you are given interavenous feeding.

Many organs in the body have ducks leading from them.

The lungs are comical in shape.

Poisonous wastes leave the body through the rectory.

When I was ill I got wonderful treatment and care in the Bone Sick Cure Hospital.

One of my greatest worries is that in my reclining years I will contact Old Timer's Disease.

I had severe pains in my stomach so I went to the doctor. After a few tests he diagnosed that I had ulsters.

I am not a great believer in alternative medicine, especially acapulco where they stick all those needles in you.

Alexander the Grate died of painful polaroids.

The Bubonic Plagiarist devastated Europe.

Mal area is spread by midget bites.

A doctor who looks after your eyes is called an optimist while a doctor who looks after your feet is called a pessimist.

I used to have difficulty controlling my spinster but I've passed a lot of water since then.

You can cure most skin complaints with an ultra-violent lamp.

Whenever I want more tablets I just ask the doctor for a new proscription.

We should all practice the art of deep breathing. First take a deep breath, hold it for five minutes and then expire.

I was a patient at the Iron Throat Hospital.

Some people break out in spots if they eat shellfish – it's a terrible allegory.

My doctor couldn't make up his mind about my condition so he insulted a specialist.

I have terrible trouble with my bladder. Sometimes it is totally incompetent.

When I was a little girl I was intoxicated against polo.

When I was in hospital it was embarrassing having my genial organs washed by the nurse.

Some health freaks have sessions of colonic irritation.

Children with fragile bones often suffer from crickets.

My sister doesn't like her looks so she's going to be treated by a drastic surgeon.

Expectant mothers should be careful of taking tablets in case they damage the unborn faeces.

If you eat meat that is out of date you run the risk of pantomime poisoning.

Gynaecologists have a busy day at the orifice.

Transcendental medication can calm your nerves.

If you get too wet you can die of ammonia.

One of my favourite artists is Michelangelo who painted the roof of the Sixteenth Chapel.

It was so quiet in the house you could hear a mouse dropping.

I've found it doesn't pay to be cheeky with traffic warders.

Red Indians live in a reservoir.

One of my favourite dishes is Beef Strong Enough.

I'd like to change my will, so I intend to ask my solicitor to add a cul de sac to it.

My son is a very saintly fellow. I feel he may even have a vacation to the priesthood.

My father worked for the government for many years. He's a senile servant.

My dog has just had a litre of puppies.

I'm buying a new car on higher perches. I've never had anything on the extortion plan before.

My son is doing wonderfully well in the army. Within a few weeks he was made a court marshal.

I remained single until I was nearly thirty. Then I entered into the state of holy acrimony.

I am often sorry I didn't follow a career in pubic administration.

44

Marrying two wives is bigotry but marrying three, tri-gonometry, is much worse. Still, either state is better than monotony.

My favourite perfume is odour cologne.

I believe there are two types of forest – carnivorous and insidious.

I hate being the skateboard for other people's mis-takes.

During the Second World War I was one of the many thousands of children evaporated to the countryside.

My washing machine has broken down because some-body threw a spaniel in the works.

I have just applied to my local health authority for a disability benefit. They sent me a bluff form to fill in.

When I was leaving the office the girls gave me a pre-sent as a momentum of the occasion.

I check prices at my local supermarket every week. I'm amazed at the way baked beans flatulate.

When I went to the hospital for an X-ray I was told to change my clothes in a cuticle.

I was at sea recently and I was lucky enough to see the fishermen catch a shawl of herrings.

Every Christmas I love to listen to the queen's speech – the vagina monologue.

My husband does not take sandwiches to work anymore. He uses luncheon vultures instead.

I was given one of those new fountain pens as a present but I never use it because I hate messing about with those cartilages.

My little nephew is always getting throat infections, so he's going in to hospital to have his asteroids removed.

I attended a wedding recently and I thought the bribe and the gloom looked wonderful.

I don't use very much makeup. But I like a little massacre on my eyes.

Sometimes for a special treat I like to give my family a special dessert – Neopolitician ice cream.

I'm always careful of dust in case I get a foreigner's body in my eye.

World War Two was an event unparalysed in human history.

My brother finds it difficult to concentrate while teaching. Sometimes he goes off on a tandem.

MY FAVOURITE NURSERY RHYMES

I loved reading these lines to my children when they were little:

London breeches falling down

Handel and Gristle

Robin Hood was attacked by the Big Bad Wolf

Diddle diddle dumpling mice on John

She cut off their tales with a carbon knife

The Pied Piper of Hamlet

There was a little girl and she had a little curl, Right in the middle of her forest

Little Miss Muffet sat on a tuffet,
Eating her curves away

The three little prigs

Walt Disney's Scampi

Dick Whittington and his Cap

Mary, Mary, quiet and hairy

One for the bastard and one for the lame

My uncle was an old soldier who rose to the rank of corpuscle.

I'm not too keen on sunbathing because of the effect of the sun's sultry violate rays.

I'm very glad to hear the miner's strike has been settled by holding a ballet at the pits.

I couldn't guess what I was getting for my birthday but I worked it out by a process of illumination.

When on holiday I always boil water before drinking it in order to putrefy it.

When I'm writing a letter I like to leave a one inch virgin all around the page.

I'll never forget the first time I met my future son-in-law. 'So you're my daughter's fiasco', I said to him.

When on holiday I like to visit the uninhibited parts of the world.

My favourite footballer was crapped for England seventeen times.

I know a man who reads the old testament all the time. He's a regular bibliomaniac.

My objection to double glazing is that it gives rise to too much compensation.

There's nothing I like more than to spend a day in the country with a full picnic hamster.

I once visited the west of Ireland and stood on the very spot where Alcock and Bull landed in their aeroplane after flying across the Atlantic.

I don't believe much of what my next door neighbour tells me. I take everything that woman says with a dose of salts.

I love my new word processor and I find the curser particularly helpful.

The first intimidation I received that I had to go to court was when a policeman knocked on my door.

Once I was taken short in the street and was forced to use a public conveyance.

I'm very particular about what kind of bed I sleep on. I always demand an inferior sprung mattress.

I'm very concerned about the damage done by topical typhoid storms.

When I found my bra was the wrong size I was utterly chestfallen.

I sometimes play a game of patients at night just to relieve the monopoly.

People often try to make an escape coat out of me for things I haven't done.

One of my greatest consolations is to have a husband to shave all the enjoyable things in life.

I've been reading about a dreadful disease called sleeping sickness brought on by the bite of the sexy fly.

Because of all the recent scares about consumer terrierism, I never buy anything in a supermarket unless it is helmetically sealed.

My artistic nephew has just got a job with a publishing firm as a poof reader.

My favourite poet is Wordsworth because he was always answering the call of nature.

My favourite religious sex is the Quackers.

I'm going to ask the chemist to give me something to get rid of the plague of aunts in my house.

I've been reading a Swedish book on sexual self exploration. Now at last I know where my volvo is.

The present government is a case of too many cooks and not enough Indians.

I really should be in hospital for all intensive purposes.

My Recent Reproductive Experiences

I was convinced I had completed my family, that I was impregnable, inconceivable and even insurmountable, and that my child baring days were over. Yet there were certain symptoms – I hadn't demonstrated for three months so I felt I might be stagnant.

So I paid a visit to the eternity hospital and the doctor who examined me told me I was in the family's way. Worse still, I was endemic because I didn't have enough red corkscrews in my bloodscream. He inscribed ironic tabloids for me but when he saw the size of my stomach he advised me to dye it. He told me that I have a cute angina but I resorted that I came to be examined not to be admired.

When it came to the time of birth the obstinate electrician advised me to have a Cistercian section but I decided to have an au naturel childbirth instead. However, when my womb was diluted and the painful contraptions started, I quickly asked for a epiduracell. As it turned out, the midwife had to use her biceps to deliver the baby. Then she cut the biblical cord.

Later, I went through the mental pause and had hot flashes. In the end, I had to have my aviaries removed and my malaproprian tubes tied. Ah, the fertility of it all.

When my grandfather joined the army many years ago he couldn't decide between the calvary and the infamy.

What sort of car do I drive? A fait accompli of course!

A FAIT ACCOMPLI

I remember as a little girl during the war listening to the radio broadcasts of Lord Hee-Haw.

My favourite Scottish poet is Rabbi Burns.

When other people point out my little verbal blunders to me, it really gets my gander up.

52

I'm thinking of writing a novel. I already have the mucus of a good plot.

I'm not really too keen on foreign men but I had no objection when my daughter became engaged to an Arab shriek with lots of money.

I have just started studying philosophy. The philosopher I admire most of all is Pluto the ancient Greek.

I do not approve of the dismissive society. I am totally opposed to all immortal behaviour.

My husband and I have decided to build a conservative beside our house.

I have just filled in my income tax form and sent it to the Inspector of Texas.

At the moment I am having some workmen in for altercations.

My husband and I think we can have our marriage nullified because it has never been consommé.

I'm very health conscious. I won't eat any food that has conservatives in it.

I must admit I'm inclined to make the odd foxes pass.

I wish technical experts would explain things in lame man's terms.

I'm very interested in the space race. I watch every launch from Cape Carnival.

I do not approve of the effluent society because they are stinking rich. Nor do I approve of people with the odour of sanctity – they stink to high heaven.

One of my favourite buildings is St Paul's cathedral designed by Sir Christopher Robin.

I have an upset stomach. I'm afraid it may be a billiards attack.

I once met the Irish prime minister, the teeshirt, or is it the toysock – I can never remember.

My daughter hasn't been able to start a family, so she's going to try artificial inspermation.

I went to the doctor with circle eight tory problems and he told me I had flea bite us.

The plumber said he would call some day next week but I wish he would be more pacific.

When my son went to America he picked up poison ivory.

I think marriage is like a prison for most women – a state of penile servitude.

More of My Religious Beliefs

I am a staunch Catholic. I believe the pope when he speaks ex-catheter.

The Mohammedan bible is called the Kodak.

An epistle is the wife of an apostle.

Martin Luther died as a result of being excommunicated by a bull.

Elijah went up to Heaven in a fiery carrot.

Psalm Sunday is a feast day when everyone sings hymns from the bible.

Jacob had a brother called See-Saw.

St Paul was converted on the road to Domestos.

The patron saint of animals is St Francis of Onassis.

Jesus should have been released instead of Brer Rabbit.

Martin Luther had a digestive upset because of a diet of worms.

Two of the Wise Men were called Frank and Sense.

The first man in the bible was called Edam.

Agnes Dei was the Mother of God.

The principal religion of China is confusionism.

Our Father, who art in Heaven, Harold be thy name.

The members of the Church of Latterday Saints are known as morons.

The pope declared Luther's teaching to be hereditary.

The Twenty Third Sam – Shirley good Mrs Murphy will follow me all the days of my life.

Lead us not into Thames Station.

The Geneva Witnesses are a religious sex.

At Pentecost, God sent us the Holy Goat.

The Utilitarian Church is of recent origin.

A seminary is where priests bury their dead.

People who are not Jews are called reptiles.

The Virgil Mary was the mother of Jesus

A vixen is the wife of a vicar.

The Authorised Virgin is the best translation of the bible.

Alias was one of the sons of Abraham.

You cannot serve God and Mamma.

They came to Jesus carrying a parable on a bed.

One of the vows monks take is a promise to celebrate.

The major religions of the world are Catholic and Prostitute.

I don't know if I'm going to Heaven, Hell or Puberty.

If I were to change my religion I would become a Seventh Day Adventurer.

My favourite saint is St Samuel A Beckett.

The apoplectic end of the world is Agamemnon.

My favourite prayer is the Angus Dei.

Noah's wife was called Joan of Ark.

One of my favourite historical characters is the Bazaar of Russia.

I have just planted some beautiful scabies flowers in my garden.

I love the flavour of orange but I find that oranges are expensive. So I often make do with consecrated orange juice instead.

I have just cut my hand on a silver of glass.

I'm due to have a serious operation, but I have every confidence in the atheist who will put me to sleep.

I took a course learning how to save people from drowning by artificial perspiration.

Before my baby was born, I attended the anti-navel clinic.

I have just been to see the octopus. He told me I have cadillacs on my eyes.

Many poets die in damp attics after a life of self-abuse.

Some children came to my door the other evening collecting for bombfires night.

Two of my favourite comedians are Rabbit and Bordello.

My daughter has just walked down the isle.

The nearest London tube station to my hotel was the Elephant and Castle.

In church one Sunday morning I complemented the

clergyman who had preached the sermoan. I told him every word of it was absolutely superfluous.

When I worked as a secretary I used to keep the minuets at meetings.

When I couldn't pay my rent I was evacuated from my house by a bayleaf.

My daughter will probably never have a baby because her husband always wears a condominium.

Some famous American authors have won the Pullet Surprise.

I feel very strongly about conservation. I'm a member of the National Truss.

When my daughter was married all the guests threw graffiti at the bride.

My husband has just bought me a waist disposal system.

I have just been elected secretary of a local organisation. My first task is to make out a gender for the opening meeting.

After my marriage, I had an exciting wedding conception.

Madame Twoswords is a famous earwax museum in London.

I just love seafood. Last time I dined out I had a portion of skimpy.

I don't like the rumours being brandied about that I drink too much.

When my friend was in hospital with a serious illness I brought her some flowers to improve her morals.

I was reading the other night about the fine mess Stanley got into on his African exploration and the famous meeting where he uttered the words 'Ken Livingstone, I presume'.

My niece hopes to become an opera singer. She plans to make her debut at Convent Garden.

I think it is disgraceful how some men live off women's immortal earnings.

My daughter first met her boyfriend in France. It was Versailles at first sight.

My little grandson had to go for therapy because he had a speech predicament.

When I was a teenager I was sent home from school with stained underwear but it was just a pigment of my menstruation.

We should always be on our guard against illnesses because some viruses can lie doormat for years.

How Shakespeare Imitated Me

I was not the first person of course to create those charming verbal blunderbusses that now bear my name. In *Much Ado About Nothing* old Bill Jakesbeer himself had a character named Dogberry who intimated me shamelessly. However, his efforts, with one notable exception, were rather connived and not very funny. It is fortunate the name did not stick or you would now be reading a book of dogberries, which sounds like some fowl K9 intestate disorder. Here, for the record, are a few of Dogberry's efforts:

You are thought here to be the most senseless and fit man for the constable of the watch.

For the watch to babble and to talk is most tolerable and not to be endured.

Adieu; be vigitant I beseech you.

Comparisons are odorous. [His best one]

Our watch sir, have indeed comprehended two auspicious persons.

It shall be suffigance.

Only get the learned writer to set down our excommunication.

By this time our sexton hath reformed Signor Leonato of the matter.

O villain! Thou wilt be condemn'd into everlasting redemption for this.

Is the whole dissembly appeared?

Dost thou not suspect my place? Dost thou not suspect my years?

And if a merry meeting may be wished, God prohibit it!

MY REVENGE ON SHAKESPEARE

One of my favourite characters in Shakespeare is Desmonda who played the trumpet in Othello's bed.

Shakespeare wrote tragedies, comedies and hysterectomies.

As one of the three witches said 'Bubble, bubble, toilet trouble'.

Beware the Brides of March.

Juliet's sirname was Catapult.

Omelette was the Prince of Denmark.

I love to go to Ascot and look at the Royal Disclosure.

I think it is dangerous to see young girls hijacking a lift on the motorway.

My favourite painting is the Moaner Wheezer.

I excuse my verbal lapses by saying I am metamorphically speaking.

I'd like to live to be a hundred years old and become a centurion.

My teenage son uses a lot of bad language but I think it's just a phrase he's going through.

I'm knitting a palaver for my nephew.

When I was younger I was hoping to marry a rich typhoon.

The chateau my husband stayed in during the war had a French widow in every bedroom.

I've go to take an examination but I don't know if it will be written or vice versa.

I went out into the night and there was a blinding gizzard.

My son is studying for a doctorate. He will soon submit his Ph.D. faeces.

I have just installed some new tubercular lighting in my house.

I went to the doctor and he told me I had sick as hell anemia as well as fireballs in my eucharist.

One of the most perplexing religious doctrines is that of the emasculate deception.

I do all my shopping at the supermarket and not at the corner shop because the prices there are very exuberant.

I used to wear pyjamas but recently I have taken to wearing a negligent.

I think air pollution is a fragrant violation of human rights.

We should all be very worried about the spectrum of the nuclear detergent hanging over the world.

At certain times of the month I get the urge to play the catarrh. It must have something to do with my minstrel cycle.

My son has gone to America but I hope to be incommunicado with him soon.

SOME OF MY FAVOURITE BOOKS AND POEMS

Lame is Rob (Victor Huge)

Donkey Hut (Manual Cervical)

The Lying Bitch in the Wardrobe (C. S. Loose)

Moby Dick and Other Tales of Semen

Thomas More's Ethiopia

Tennyson's In Memorandum

Freddy the Rabbit Slept Late

Don Coyote

Jason and the Hunt for the Golden Fleas

Coleridge's Ku Klux Klan

The Deserted Traveller (Oliver Goldberg)

Last of the Moccasins (J. Pennymore Cooper)

Wordsworth's Imitations of Immorality

Homer's Simpson

I wandered lonely as a cow (Wordsworth)

They have slain the Earl of Moray, And Lady Monde-green.

Gullible's Travels (Jonathan Twit)

The mother of Achilles dipped him in the River Stynx until he was intolerable.

Every Christmas my church holds a bizarre sale of work.

The highlight of my marriage ceremony was when my husband was asked 'Do you take this woman to be your awful wedded wife?'

My son works for the ministry of defence. His job is to keep the fence painted.

My favourite brand of biscuits is McBitties.

I saw this very interesting film once about a dwarf who lived in a German I.O.U. camp – he was a Stalag-mite.

I can't milk a cow – I leave that to udders.

My unmarried daughter is expecting a baby. I'm not passing any judgement until I hear her virgin of the story.

At first I didn't think I could have children because my husband was quite impudent.

When I visited Australia recently, the animals I like most were the cola bears and the aubergines.

My favourite fast food is hamburglars.

I believe that the cotton crop in the US Deep South is ruined by the bold weasel.

Some of my favourite flowers are coronations.

One of my teenage nephews has acme all over his face.

I'd love to have a quaint old house with ivory growing up the walls.

When I'm in town there is nothing I like more than to have lunch and a glass of wine in a brassiere.

At my daughter's wedding, she displayed her new 22-carrot gold ring.

One of my favourite poets is Keats and my very favourite line is 'Season of mists and melon fruitfulness'.

My son was married in an old-fashioned ceremony. He said to his wife-to-be, 'To thee I pledge my trough!'

When you eat, your food passes through your elementary canal.

When I go to an expensive restaurant, there is nothing I like better than a dish of roast peasant.
MMMM!
SAUCE
PEASANT MUSTARD

The highest peak in the Alps is Blanc Mange.

The French national anthem is the mayonnaise.

The Awful Tower is in Paris.

In France you can have fuel coal de sack or à la carte.

French people live in gateaux.

French cities are full of burglars.

French houses are made of plaster of Paris.

'Pa de deux' means 'Father of Twins'.

Inhabitants of the French capital are usually called parasites.

'Coup de grâce' is French for 'mow the lawn'.

I love to have Horse's Doovers before a meal.

The Pyramids are mountains between France and Spain.

The French Underground consisted mostly of conni-sewers.

If you ask a French child if he wants to use the toilet he will say 'Oui, oui'.

My Love Affair with Italy

There is a famous leaning tower in Pizza.

Glaziers slide down the Alps.

People in Venice travel in gorgonzolas.

An Italian baby is called a bamboo.

My favourite Italian film star is Gina Lollobrigadier.

Italy lies in the temperance zone.

Malt and larva run down the sides of Mount Edna.

Florence and nipples are close together.

At the south end of Italy is the island of Cecily.

In the north of Italy is the river Poo.

Italian police are called cabin attendants.

Pompeii was destroyed by an overflow of saliva from the Vatican.

The streets of Venus are completely flooded.

I was reading in the newspapers how robbers stole a huge amount of gold billion.

I've taken up sailing so I've bought a dingy boat.

I was delighted to learn that one of the most popular Christian names in Poland is Santa Claus.

My son has had hundreds of girlfriends. He's a regular Casablanca.

I think that life is hard and we must take nothing for granite.

I'm having dental trouble so I intend to get some fal-setto teeth.

My friend is seriously ill. The doctors have diagnosed double ammonia.

When I went to visit the doctor, the first thing he did was to feel my purse.

My brother has just go a job in a vegetable market at a celery of 30,000 a year.

I think the unclear arms race should end. For a start there should be a ban on the production of geranium.

I love watching wrestling and judy on TV.

I admit I am pretty fat, but I don't agree with my doctor when he says I'm obeast.

I was once the chairman at a meeting which became so rowdy that I had to band my gravel.

For name tags I always use incredible ink.

I just hate cruelty to animals. If animals have to be killed, it should be done with a human killer.

My grandfather could neither read nor write. He was completely illegitimate.

I went to a restaurant one night but I found that the food was completely indelible.

No man should have more than one wife. I support mahogany.

I have inconvertible evidence about the identity of Jack the Ripper.

The first time I saw a snake I was absolutely putrefied.

One of the highlights of my trip to Russia was a visit to the gremlin.

My two neighbours are always at it hammer and tongues.

MY FAVOURITE BOOKS
AND
LITERARY CHARACTERS

Withering Heights

Gray's Allergy

Shakespeare's Merry Widow

Touchdown in As You Like It

Tess of the Dormobiles

Robinson Caruso

The Scarlet Litter

Long John Hitler

Virgil's Aniseed

Orwell's Dining Out in London and Paris

Fellatio – Hamlet's best friend

Milton's Paradise Lust

Shelley's Ode to a Skylight

Darwin's Organ of the Spices

Tolkien's Habit

Homer's Oddity

Laurence of A Rabies

Gray's Effigy

Romeo and Juliet – the heroic couplet

101 Damnations

The Little Louse on the Dreary

Agatha Christie's Witness for the Prostitution

Pope's Heroic Cutlets

The Honky-Tonk Expedition

The Count of Monte Carlo

James Joyce's Useless

Cot on a Hot Tin Roof

Robinson's Caruso's Good Friday

Adolph Hitler's Mine Cramp

The Middle of March by Jumbo Elliot

Charles Dickens' The Old Courtesy Shop

I think my husband is just a
bit too amorous. In fact, I feel
he's a sex-mechanic.

My brother was an attaché case at the French embassy.

I'm not a very good chess player. I don't even know how to move my prawns.

One of the most valuable lessons I learned in school was 'never end a sentence with a proposition'.

One night I was attacked by a mugger, but I kept my composer throughout the incident.

I often get this strange feeling that great events are about to happen. I think it must be sidekick.

I heard my grandson at prayer the other night: 'Lead a snot into temptation'.

I was looking for legal representation so I picked a lawyer at ransom in the phone book.

My nephew was displaying some strange symptoms so they took him to the doctor. He was diagnosed as being artistic.

When I went to Egypt, I saw the stinks in the dessert.

I had a severe inflection recently so the doctor injected me with peninsula.

When I was travelling through the jungle I was attacked by a boa constructor.

While I am on the beach there is nothing I like more than to see sunbathers basketing in the sun.

I picked up my latest outfit at a Rembrandt sale.

I really miss the company of my recently diseased husband.

One of my favourite dishes is roast lion of pork.

I'm really looking forward to reading the latest government wipe paper.

My son was recently attacked by a mugger and beaten subconscious.

My telephone broke down recently so I had to use the chaos in the village.

My nephew has just got a job at the airport. He's in the customs and exercise division.

I've recently visited an art gallery where I saw all the mantelpieces of the great masters.

One of my favourite moments of the political year is when the government presents its budgie to the nation.

When I got married I wanted some time off work to go on my honeymoon. So I applied for passionate leave.

American criminals are often incastrated in Sing Song penitentiary.
SING SONG

My Knowledge of Geography

The Mediterranean and the Red Sea are connected by the Sewage Canal.

The fields in Egypt are irritated by the Nile.

The equator is a menagerie lion running around the middle of the earth.

America was discovered by Columbanus.

The Urinal mountains are in Russia.

Hot parts of the world are called the horrid zones.

The people of the frozen north are called equinoxes.

It is very hot and wet in the topical regions of the world.

The people of Malta are called Maltesers.

The abdominal snowman is found in Tibet.

Separating North and South America is the Pyjama Canal.

My grandfather used to live in Bury Street, Edmunds.

The Faroes were islands in ancient Egypt.

My favourite memory of my recent trip to Spain was the display of flamingo dancing.

I'm sorry I never took a holiday in the Soviet Onion while it still existed.

Oriental people like to ride around in jigsaws.

In Scandinavia, they put omelettes over some letters of the alphabet.

Switzerland is famous for the invention of condemned milk.

The capital of Norway is Oxo.

A sultan keeps all his wives in Harlem.

For many years Russia lay hidden behind the ironed curtain.

In 1972, the United States Space Agency made a lunatic landing.

Grease is just a spot on the map.

Canada has many wide open spaces. The country is very sparsely copulated.

Some South American countries are just bandana republics.

The Vampire State Building is in New York.

The Great Wall of China was built to keep out the Mongrel hordes.

The four seasons are salt, pepper, vinegar and mustard.

Albanians have white hair and pink eyes.

The path of the earth around the sun is an eclipse.

The earth makes a resolution every twenty-four hours.

Much of the world's rubber is produced in malaria.

The inhabitants of Moscow are called mosquitoes.

Plasticine is a country in the Middle East.

The seaport of Athens is called the pyorrhoea.

The world's biggest sea is the Specific Ocean.

The line around the middle of the earth is called the creator.

Manila is the capital of the Philistines.

Milligan was the first man to sail around the world.

In India people are divided into casts and outcasts.

The rubble is the unit of currency in Russia.

Japanese girls dress in commodes.

In Greece, nude bathing is allowed on the pubic beaches.

Columbus circumcised the world with a forty foot clipper.

At the Tower of London, the Beefburgers hold halibuts in their hands.

In China a lot of vases date from the Ming Dysentery.

Marie and Toinette first said 'Let them have their cake and eat it'.

SuDoku is sweeping the country like wild flowers.

I think women should have equal sex for equal pay for equal work.

I've always had a wonderful repertoire with my children.

I'm very afraid of floods, earthquakes, and other catechisms of nature.

I saw a very exciting film on TV the other night where a prehistoric caveman was attacked by a giant thesaurus.

A neighbour's dog has just attacked my little grandson. This is the sort of thing that must be nipped in the butt.

Too many women authors seem to be joining the ranks of the cliterati these days.

I'm told I have an above average HQ. I'm hoping to join Densa.

The twins are very alike – just like two peas in a pot.

I'm having a blood test and I'm very worried in case I turn out to be VIP positive.

I'm very afraid my husband may die suddenly so I've just taken out one of those endearment policies for him.

I cannot take sugar in any shape or form. I'm diabolic.

I've just been reading in the newspaper that the police have just uncovered a huge catch of Carmelite rifles.

My eldest son teaches at the university. He's a lecherer in sociology.

My Historical Knowledge

Daniel O'Connell was responsible for Catholic constipation.

Louis XIV was the first king to declare 'Le Twat, c'est moi'.

Mussolini's followers were facetious.

Mary Queen of Snots married the Dolphin of France.

The constitution of the United States gave everyone the right to bare arms.

The German emperor was called the Geyser.

Anne Berlin was the wife of Henry VIII.

Francis Drake said the Armada could wait but his bowels couldn't.

Louis XVI was gelatined in the French Resolution.

Florence Nightingale sang in Ber Kelly Square.

Napoleon said that England was a nation of shoplifters.

Henry the Eighth's marriage was dull and void.

Marco Polo was Master of the Mint.

Napoleon was imprisoned on the isle of Melba and later in St Helen's.

Cleopatra was stung by a poisonous wasp.

Anne of Cloves was married to Henry the Ape (also Catherine of Arrogance).

Napoleon was defeated by the Duck of Wellington.

The Battle of Waterloo was won by Duke Ellington.

Even Napoleon had his Watergate.

The motto of the French Revolution was Liberty, Equality, Maternity.

One of the most famous kings of England was William the Conjuror.

Napoleon had no children because Josephine was a baroness.

Victoria was the longest serving souvenir England ever had.

Magna Carta – she did not die in vain.

The Crusaders overcame the Saccharins.

I cannot swallow anything at the moment because my throat is in flames.

My brother is a diabetic because his St Pancras has ceased to function.

Because of my fame, there are plans to put a plague on my house.

At my wedding, I carried a bucket of my favourite flowers – enemas.

My favourite reading gender is science friction.

I once ate two dozen oysters and got selfish poisoning.

When I found a fly in my soup in a restaurant I naturally complained to the manager. He told me it must have committed insecticide.

I was watching a pirate film on TV the other night. I saw a gunboat fire a warning shot across the bowels.

When my husband returned home from the pub last night he was completely gincoherent.

I do not approve of the arms race or the incontinent ballistic missals.

My husband died intestine without a will.

I'm an enthusiastic music follower. I never miss the Last Night of the Poms.

If I were on television, I bet I would win an Enema award.

My daughter has completed her family so she is going to have a tubal litigation.

I'm a sport's widow. My husband never leaves the golf curse.

I've been reading about a Japanese business man who got into financial difficulties. He committed cash and carry.

I was driving home the other night when the police stopped me and asked me to blow into a brotheliser.

I'm very proud of my grandson. He's just been made a perfect at his school.

I'll never forget the things my late lamentable father said to me.

I have just bought an expensive new table made entirely of monogamy.

One of the happiest memories of my courtship is sitting on a couch canoeing with my boyfriend.

When cooking I use a lot of desecrated coconut.

The Irish parliament is called
the Dole.

Sodhim Insane is the most notorious leader ever to come out of a rack.

I hated the system of government in South Africa based on skin colour. I've always been an opponent of apart hide.

John Lennon was a famous Russian politician, as was Joe Stallion.

Chinese politicians have frequent erections.

The British prime minister lives at Number Ten, Drowning Street.

The best president of the United States was PLJ.

George Bush is undergoing his second term of pregnancy.

The president of Cuba is Fidel Castrato.

Franklin Delaney Roosevelt was US president.

Doctors are producing new inflammation on arthritis all the time.

I distrust doctors so I am consulting a fake healer.

If I'm feeling happy in the morning, I always slide down the barristers.

My husband was so good on our honeymoon I gave him a standing ovulation.

I love putting explanation marks at the end of a sentence.

I was given a present of a beautiful new dress. It's covered with thousands of sequences.

The snack I like best is cream cheese with a beagle.

One of my favourite historical authors is the Venereal Bede.

The football team I follow was recently regulated from the Premier Division.

One of my favourite books of reference is Roger's Brontosaurus.

I have just required a new dog – a datsun.

In ancient times, people used to wear omelettes around their necks to ward off evil spirits.

My cousin is a sealiac and has to have a glutton free diet.

I have to go to the hospital to get a sex ray.

At my daughter's wedding her bouquet was a bunch of friesians.

One of my favourite jazz singers is Elephants Gerald.

I've been reading the latest murder sadistics in the papers.

Before a list of candidates for a job is interviewed, the screaming committee have to make a blacklist.

I'm very upset because the interest rate on my bank loan has risen to twenty per cent per anum.

When I have a digestive upset I always take Milk of Amnesia.

I'm fed up of making beds so I'm getting rid of all my blankets and buying bidets instead.

In church, I cannot hear a word of the sermon because of the poor quality of the agnostics.

My father was injured during the war when he was hit by a piece of sharpnel.

My lazy son just sits there all day doing that puzzle in the newspaper, the sad blokeu.

My favourite scene in Hamlet is where Polonius gets stabbed in the arse.

Scientists should be given as much money as they need to build large lavatories in which they can do important work.

A bishop wears a metre on his head.

My son was seriously ill in hospital so they put him in expensive care.

In the stomach your food gets mixed up with the ghastly juices.

A gentleman is someone who gives up his seat to a lady in a public convenience.

I'm going to have my house redesigned from top to bottom so I have enlisted the services of an inferior decorator.

My father was a man of great statue.

I love the Spanish national anthem 'Jose can you see ...'

I just bought a huge new motor boat. It goes twenty miles to the galleon.

I like to travel on the railway notwork.

Some of my remarks are a bit tangenital.

My Favourite Theatre and Films

John Millicent Sing's Ploughboy of the Western World

Shakespeare's Titus and Ronicus (The Two Gentlemen of Verona)

Peter Cook and Dudley Moore's Beyond the Fridge

Captain Corelli's Mandarin

The Admiral Crichton

She Stoops to Conga

Arsenal and Old Lace

Dancing at Lufthansa

King Leer and his daughter Gonorrhea

Joxer, the whole world is in a state of chassis

Butch Cassidy and Some Damn Kid

Horse and Wells, the famous film star

Colostomy Jane

A Sidecar Named Desire

The Importance of Being Ear Nest (Oxter Wilde)